The material in this book does not constitute medical advice. It is intended for informational purposes only. The authors take no responsibility for the reader following the information in this book. Please consult your doctor for specific treatment recommendations regarding your specific renal diet. Before taking any course of treatment, please seek the advice of a physician or health care provider.

The following recipes are specific for Chronic Kidney Disease (CKD). Due to variations in ingredients, the nutritional analyses should be used as guidelines and we cannot guarantee the accuracy of all values.

Introduction

With 30 years of nursing behind me and being a Mom to two wonderful boys, I decided it was time to collaborate with my niece, whose mother suffers from ESRD, in writing this wonderful cookbook for people living with Kidney Disease. Now let's read a little background on what Kidney Disease is and why eating right is oh-so important.

Chronic Kidney Disease also called CKD, means that the kidneys are not working effectively. What this means is that one or both of the kidneys have been damaged, and in most cases overtime these organs will completely stop functioning. The kidneys are an essential part of our body. They removing waste, balance fluids, remove drugs from our blood, control blood pressure, influence the production of our red blood cells, and produce Vitamin D for your bones. Suffice to say, these organs are extremely important.

The best line of defense in helping yourself is of course, making good life choices. This means eating a healthy kidney-friendly diet, exercising, not smoking, and maintaining a healthy weight. Extra weight causes undue stress on your kidneys, as well as your heart by making them work harder. Salt should be decreased, if not eliminated, to keep your blood pressure within a good range. Potassium is a mineral found in many foods. Excess potassium impairs nerves and causes numbness and tingling and can also cause muscle weakness. This is very important for the heart, as excess potassium, can cause heart failure. Phosphorous is also a mineral found in foods. Along with potassium, these minerals are not removed from the blood effectively when kidney disease is present. Excess phosphorous causes itching of the skin, and pulls calcium from the bones, making them brittle and weak.

Renal diets vary according to your dietician or your physician's orders... but a typical diet will contain in a one day period... 2000 mg. sodium, 2000 mg. potassium, 1000 mg. phosphorous, and 60 gm. protein.

Our kidneys help discharge metabolic wastes and toxins as well as too much water from the body. Impaired kidneys, as in CKD, need help to maintain optimum kidney functioning. This is usually accomplished by developing a personalized renal diet with your doctor and dietitian. We hope that this cookbook will give you tons of inspiration and show you that you can still eat delicious foods even on a restricted diet.

Table Of Contents

Understanding A Few Renal Key Words

A list of important terminology in understanding Chronic Kidney Disease

Kidney: One of two bean-shaped organs that create urine by filtering waste from the blood.

Creatinine: This is a waste product of the wear and tear of muscles of the body...the level of creatinine in the blood rises as kidney disease progresses.

Urea: A waste product that is eliminated by the kidneys.

Proteinuria: Protein in the urine...If the kidneys cannot hold onto the protein the body needs, they will leak it into the urine. High protein in the urine is significant of kidney problems.

BUN: A blood test used to measure the amount of urea in the blood.

Glomerulus: A tiny set of looping blood vessels in the kidneys where blood is filtered.

GFR or glomerular filtration rate: This is a blood test to see how well the kidneys are filtering waste and excess fluid from the blood. The normal value (varies with weight and age) ranges around 90 or above....a GFR below 60 means kidney problems....below 15 means dialysis or transplant is needed.

There are 5 stages of kidney Disease ranging from 1 meaning normal kidney filtration...2 is a mild decrease in filtration...3 is a moderate decrease in filtration...4 is a severe decrease in filtration and 5 is kidney failure.

ESRD: End Stage Renal Disease...Total kidney failure

Dialysis: The process of cleaning waste products from the blood artificially.

Leaching or Dialyzing

Potatoes, carrots, sweet potatoes, and beets are a staple in many diets. It is hard enough to eat a renal diet without eliminating such hearty vegetables. Leaching the veggies can pull some of the potassium out of them, but be careful and check with your dietician as to how much is OK on your diet.

1. Peel and slice the veggie into small pieces.

2. Using 10 times the amount of water per amount of veggie, soak the veggies for 2 hours.

3. Drain and repeat process of soaking.

4. Cook with 5 times the amount of water to the amount of veggie.

List Of Foods To Avoid

High Sodium Foods

Salts, bottled sauces (soy sauce, teriyaki sauce, some barbecue sauces, oyster sauce, gravies, etc.) cured meats (hot dogs, canned meats, bacon, sausage, luncheon meats) snacks (chips with salt, crackers, candy) frozen prepared dinners, packaged meals

High Potassium Foods

Citrus fruits, avocadoes, apricots, pomegranates, nectarines, papaya, mangoes, bananas, melons, lentil, potatoes (unleached), artichokes, bamboo shoots, Chinese cabbage, cooked spinach, cooked broccoli, brussel sprouts, milk, bran, chocolate, molasses, nuts, peanut butter, some cereals

High Phosphorous Foods

Beer, cocoa, yogurt, brewer's yeast, baked beans, chick peas, kidney beans, black beans, sardines, organ meats, crayfish, oysters

Top Healthy Foods
For People with CKD

Cabbage:
½ cup = 6 mg. sodium
60 mg. potassium
9 mg.phosphorus

Cauliflower (Cooked):
½ cup = 9 mg. sodium
88 mg. potassium
20 mg.phosphorus

Red Bell Peppers:
½ cup = 9 mg. sodium
88 mg. potassium
10 mg. phosphorus

Garlic:
½ cup = 1 mg. sodium
12 mg. potassium
4 mg. phosphorous

Onions:
½ cup = 3 mg. sodium
116 mg. potassium
3 mg. phosphorous

Radishes:
½ cup = 0 mg. sodium
30 mg. potassium
0 mg. phosphorous

Asparagus (cooked):
½ cup = 12 mg. sodium
200 mg. potassium
40 mg. phosphorous

Blueberries:
½ cup = 4 mg. sodium
65 mg. potassium
7 mg. phosphorous

Cherries:
½ cup = 0 mg. sodium
160 mg. potassium
15 mg. phosphorous

Olive oil:
1 tbsp. = 1 mg. sodium
1 mg. potassium
0 mg. phosphorous

Spirulina: 1 oz. fresh
30 mg.sodium
35 mg. potassium
0 mg. phosphorous

A Few Notes...
limit hard cheese such as parmesan, mozzarella, dry-curd cottage cheese, to 3 ounces per week unless contraindicated by your dietitian.
Milk is usually limited to 8 ounces per day but I prefer Rice milk....and finally limit broccoli, corn, green peas, and mushrooms.

Spice Up Your Diet

Giving up salt does not mean giving up flavor! With herbs and spices you can season your food for an exciting new flavor.
Try the following spices with the foods listed:

Spice	Use With
Allspice	Beef, seafood, vegetables and fruit
Dill	Beef, chicken, vegetables and in dips
Ginger	Beef, chicken, vegetables and eggplant
Sage	Chicken, pork, eggplant and in dressing
Basil	Beef, pork and most vegetables
Caraway	Beef, pork, green beans, cauliflower, cabbage, asparagus and dips and marinades
Bay Leaf	Beef, pork and most vegetables
Marjoram	Beef, chicken, pork, vegetables and eggplant
Cardamom	Fruit and baked goods
Rosemary	Chicken, pork, vegetables and eggplant

Tarragon	Fish, asparagus, cabbage, cauliflower and in marinades
Curry	Beef, chicken, pork, fish, vegetables and in marinades
Thyme	Beef, chicken, pork, fish and vegetables

Other Suggestions ...

Food	Types Of Spices
Fruit	Allspice, cinnamon, cloves, mint, cardamom, ginger and nutmeg
Vegetables	Allspice, anise seed, cardamom, cinnamon, cloves, cumin, dill, ginger, tarragon, and basil
Fish	Cumin, basil, chives, fennel, dried mustard, garlic, dill, ginger, oregano, paprika, saffron, tarragon and thyme
Potatoes, (leached)	Basil, cayenne, curry, dill, horseradish, oregano, paprika, rosemary and tarragon
Eggs	Basil, chili powder, cumin, curry, dill, marjoram, paprika, tarragon and thyme
Poultry	Coriander, allspice, basil, garlic, cumin, curry, dill, ginger, marjoram, dried mustard, paprika, rosemary, saffron
Beef	Coriander, basil, garlic, parsley cumin, horseradish, marjoram, dried mustard, oregano, paprika, rosemary

How to Make Dry Cottage Cheese

I reference using dry-curd cottage cheese in many of my recipes. Dry cottage cheese...also known as dry curd cheese or cheese curds or farmer's cheese is cottage cheese without any liquid additives such as milk or cream after the milk is curdled. Finding dry curd cheese isn't easy, but you will probably have luck at the farmer's market. Another option is to rinse and drain excess liquid from store- bought cottage cheese. Also, you can use the following recipe to make dry cottage cheese from scratch. Start this process early in the day to allow time to finish. Refrigerate and use cheese within one week or wrap tightly and freeze.

Ingredients:
1 gallon milk (skim or whole)
1 cup buttermilk
½ cup instant non-fat dry milk
Cheese cloth

Directions:
1. Pour the gallon milk into lg. pot on stove.
2. Add the dry milk.
3. Cook the mixture on med-high til lukewarm.
4. Stir while adding cup of buttermilk.
5. Simmer for 12 hours until cheese curds have formed.

Breakfast

Cream Of Wheat Apple Muffins

- 1 cup flour
- 1 cup dry cream of wheat
- ½ cup sugar
- ½ cup milk (2%)
- ½ cup applesauce
- ¼ cup canola oil
- 2 egg whites

- 1 tsp. vanilla
- 1 tsp. cream of tartar
- ¼ tsp. baking soda

Directions

Prep Time: 10 min. | Cook Time: 15 min. | Servings: 12

1. In large bowl, combine all ingredients until moistened.
2. Fill paper lined muffin tins ¾ full with batter.
3. Bake in oven for 15 minutes or until toothpick inserted in center of muffin comes out clean.
4. Remove from oven and cool muffins on wire stands.

Nutrition Facts
(per serving)

Calories: 63.5
Protein: 0.4g
Sodium: 5.4mg
Phosphorus: 0.8mg
Potassium: 110.4mg

Happy Kidney Tip:
This is a refreshing summer drink made with fresh pineapple.... delicious with a zing of bubbly ginger ale.

Sweet Matzo Brei

- 4 lg. eggs
- 1 cup milk (2%)
- 1 tsp. sugar
- 4 sheets matzo
- 2 tbsp. unsalted butter
- cinnamon sugar for garnish
- raspberries for garnish

Directions

Prep Time: 5 min. | Cook Time: 5 min. | Servings: 4

1. Beat the eggs, 1 tbsp. milk, and sugar in a large bowl.
2. In another bowl, crush the matzo into small pieces.
3. Add the rest of the milk to the matzo and mix well.
4. Let stand for 2 minutes.
5. Combine the 2 bowls into one.
6. In a saucepan, melt the butter.
7. Add the matzo-egg mixture and cook, stirring continuously, until eggs barely set, around 2 minutes.
8. Serve garnished with crushed raspberries or cinnamon sugar (or both, as I did).

Nutrition Facts
(per serving)

Calories: 228.4
Protein: 11.2g
Sodium: 137.4mg
Phosphorus: 18.4mg
Potassium: 193.9mg

Happy Kidney Tip:
This heartwarming bowl is a classic Jewish breakfast and very kidney-friendly!

Kidney Cleanser Juice

- 4 stalks washed celery

- 3 sprigs parsley

- 3 sprigs coriander

- 1 cucumber

- 1/2 cup watermelon

- 1 tsp. fresh lemon juice

- 1 cup crushed ice

Directions

Prep Time: 10 min. | Cook Time: - | Servings: 4

1. Place all ingredients into blender and puree until smooth.
2. Serve and Enjoy!

Nutrition Facts
(per serving)

Calories: 50
Protein: 0.0g
Sodium: 0.0mg
Phosphorus: 9.0mg
Potassium: 96.0mg

Happy Kidney Tip:
This is excellent for your kidney health! Freeze leftover "slush" in freezer trays and use cubes in your water later.

Aloha Cocktail

- 1 cup fresh pineapple cubes

- 1 lime cut in half and juiced

- 1/2 cup ginger ale

- ice cubes

Directions

Prep Time: 10 min. | Cook Time: - | Servings: 2

1. Place pineapple, lime juice, and ginger ale in blender.
2. Blend til smooth.
3. Pour into glass filled with ice.

.

Nutrition Facts
(per serving)

Calories: 63.5
Protein: 0.4g
Sodium: 5.4mg
Phosphorus: 0.8mg
Potassium: 110.4mg

Happy Kidney Tip:
This is a refreshing summer drink made with fresh pineapple.... delicious with a zing of bubbly ginger ale.

Pancakes and Berries

- 2 large eggs
- 1 1/4 cup rice milk
- 2 tsp. vanilla extract
- 3 tbsp. canola oil
- 1 1/2 cup all purpose flour
- 1 tsp. cream of tartar
- 1/2 tsp. baking soda
- 3/4 cup blueberries
- 3/4 cup sliced strawberries

Directions

Prep Time: 10 min. | Cook Time: 10 min. | Servings: 10

1. In a large bowl, beat together the eggs, milk, and vanilla until light and foamy.
2. Add oil, flour, cream of tartar, and baking soda and stir just to combine.
3. On a greased skillet, drop batter by spoonfuls on medium heat.
4. Cook about 2 minutes on each side until pancakes are golden brown.
5. Serve with berries.

Nutrition Facts
(per serving)

Calories: 136.4
Protein: 3.2g
Sodium: 40.0mg
Phosphorus: 7.7mg
Potassium: 163.1mg

Happy Kidney Tip:
Pancakes are such a treat and are especially delightful with fresh, seasonal berries. My blueberry sauce would also be delicious on this comforting breakfast.

Apple-Stuffed Crepes

- 4 egg yolks
- 2 large eggs
- 1/4 cup sugar
- 1 cup flour
- 2 cups milk
- 2 tbsp. canola oil

Apple Filling:

- 4 apples peeled, cored, and sliced
- 1/2 cup brown sugar
- 1/2 tsp. cinnamon
- 1/2 stick butter
- dash of nutmeg

Directions

Prep Time: 10 min. | Cook Time: 10 min. | Servings: 4

1. In a medium saucepan on low heat, cook the ingredients for the filling.
2. In a large bowl mix the eggs, flour, sugar and milk.
3. Heat the oil in a medium skillet on medium heat.
4. Using a ladle, spoon some of the batter on the pan, then swirl the pan to spread the batter thinly on the bottom of the pan.
5. Cook the crepe for 20 seconds, then flip with a rubber spatula, and cook other side for 20 seconds.
6. Repeat until batter is gone.
7. Fill the crepes with a tbsp. of apple filling and roll into a log.
8. Top with additional apple filling if desired.

Nutrition Facts
(per serving)

Calories: 315
Protein: 5.0g
Sodium: 356.0mg
Phosphorus: 103.0mg
Potassium: 160.0mg

Happy Kidney Tip:
This can be spectacular to wake up to. Make the crepes the day before, assemble in the morning and warm in the oven...mmm-mmm!

Sophisticated French Toast

- 1 cup egg substitute
- 1/2 cup milk
- 3 tbsp. sugar
- 1/4 tsp. nutmeg
- 1 tsp. vanilla
- 1/2 tsp. rum extract
- 12 slices white bread

- powdered sugar

Directions

Prep Time: 1 hr. | Cook Time: 15 min. | Servings: 6

1. In a medium bowl whisk together eggs, milk, sugar, nutmeg, vanilla, and rum extract.
2. Pour mixture over bread in a sheet pan and let bread absorb egg mixture for 1 hour.
3. Place egg bread on greased griddle and cook on medium heat until golden brown.
4. Serve warm sprinkled with powdered sugar.

Nutrition Facts
(per serving)

Calories: 252
Protein: 10.0g
Sodium: 390.0mg
Phosphorus: 83.0mg
Potassium: 219.0mg

Happy Kidney Tip:
Prepare this for a sweet feast on a restful Sunday. Splurge and serve French toast with blueberry caramel sauce. (pg. 135)

Crock Pot Oatmeal

- 1 cup steel-cut oats
- 2 cups apple juice
- 2 cups rice milk
- 2 apples peeled, cored, and cut into chunks
- 1/4 cup brown sugar
- 1 tsp. cinnamon
- dash grated nutmeg
- 1/4 cup seedless grapes

Directions

Prep Time: 10 min. | Cook Time: 4 hrs. | Servings: 4

1. Place all the ingredients in the slow cooker and cook on low for 4 hours.
2. Occasionally stir the oatmeal while cooking.
3. If too thick add water and serve with any desired toppings.

Nutrition Facts
(per serving)

Calories: 336.8
Protein: 6.8g
Sodium: 50.0mg
Phosphorus: 0.9mg
Potassium: 245.1mg

Happy Kidney Tip:
This breakfast has all the flavors of apple pie with the bonus of cinnamon, which helps regulate blood sugar.

Mini Waffles and Eggs

- 1 carton egg-white product

- 1/2 cup dry-curd cottage cheese

- 20 mini toaster waffles

- 1 tbsp. butter

- pepper to taste

Directions

Prep Time: 5 min. | Cook Time: 8 min. | Servings: 5

1. Melt butter in skillet on med-low heat.
2. Add eggs and scramble until cooked.
3. Remove from heat and add cottage cheese and mix well.
4. Place eggs on top of waffles and serve.

Nutrition Facts
(per serving)

Calories: 328
Protein: 17.6g
Sodium: 720mg
Phosphorus: 30.0mg
Potassium: 85.3mg

Happy Kidney Tip:
Use only white flour, low sodium waffles when purchasing this item. These are fun to eat and pop right into your mouth!

Breakfast Bonanza

- 1 loaf french bread
- 1 1/2 cups egg substitute
- 1/2 cup pineapple juice
- 1 tbsp. vanilla extract
- 2 cups sliced strawberries
- 1 cup blueberries
- 1 cup grapes

- powdered sugar

Directions

Prep Time: 15 min. | Cook Time: 20 min. | Servings: 10

1. Pre-heat oven to 350°F.
2. Cut a loaf of French bread into 1 inch slices.
3. In a mixing bowl combine eggs, juice and vanilla extract.
4. Dip bread into mixture, coating both sides, and allowing excess to drip off.
5. Place dipped bread on lined baking sheet.
6. Cover bread and refrigerate overnight. In morning uncover bread.
7. Bake in pre-heated oven for 20 minutes or until bread is golden brown.
8. Serve with fruit and powdered sugar.

Nutrition Facts
(per serving)

Calories: 110
Protein: 5.9g
Sodium: 221.6mg
Phosphorus: 54.7mg
Potassium: 119.9mg

Happy Kidney Tip:
Egg whites are high-quality proteins with all the essential amino acids.

Apple Pie French Toast

- 2 granny-smith apples peeled, cored, and sliced
- 2 tbsp. butter
- 2 tbsp. brown sugar
- 1 tsp. flour
- 1/2 tsp. cinnamon
- 1/4 cup water
- 2 eggs

- 1/4 cup milk
- 1/2 tsp. vanilla
- 4 slices white bread

Directions

Prep Time: 10 min. | Cook Time: 10 min. | Servings: 2

1. Simmer the apples, butter, sugar, flour, cinnamon, and water in a small saucepan for 15 minutes.
2. In a wide dish, mix eggs, milk, and vanilla.
3. Dip the bread in the egg mixture and coat on both sides.
4. Melt the butter in a griddle and fry the bread 3-4 minutes on each side.
5. Serve the French toast covered in the caramelized apples.

Nutrition Facts
(per serving)

Calories: 365.9
Protein: 11.7g
Sodium: 429.3mg
Phosphorus: 18.1mg
Potassium: 378.0mg

Happy Kidney Tip:
A decadently scrumptious breakfast!

Melon-Mint Refresher

- 3 cups diced watermelon
- 1 cup strawberries
- 2 tbsp. lime juice
- 1 tbsp. sugar
- 1 cup crushed ice
- 2 sprigs mint

Directions

Prep Time: 15 min. | Cook Time: - | Servings: 4

1. Place all ingredients in a blender.
2. Pulse until smooth.

Nutrition Facts
(per serving)

Calories: 93.5
Protein: 1.2g
Sodium: 25.1mg
Phosphorus: 2.8mg
Potassium: 323.2mg

Happy Kidney Tip: Watermelon represents summer's freshness. This is a cool, soothing drink, but watch your fluid intake.

Lunch

Fragrant Egg Fried Rice

- 1 stalk lemongrass
- 1 cup basmati rice
- 1 tbsp. olive oil
- 1 green onion sliced
- 1 inch piece of ginger peeled, chopped fine
- 1 1/2 tsp. coriander seeds
- 1 1/2 tsp. cumin seeds
- 2 cups low-sodium vegetable stock
- 1/4 cup chopped cilantro
- 1 diced red pepper
- 1 beaten

Directions

Prep Time: 10 min. | Cook Time: 20 min. | Servings: 4

1. Finely chop the peeled lemongrass.
2. Rinse the rice in cold water and drain through a sieve.
3. Heat the oil in a large stockpot and add the lemongrass, spices, ginger and onion.
4. Cook for 3 minutes stirring continuously.
5. Add the rice and cook 1 more minute, stirring frequently.
6. Add the stock and bring to a boil.
7. Cover pan and simmer 18 minutes or until rice is not crunchy.
8. Remove from heat and fluff with a fork.
9. Add cilantro.

Nutrition Facts
(per serving)

Calories: 105.4
Protein: 2.7g
Sodium: 23.2mg
Phosphorus: 4.5mg
Potassium: 48.9mg

Happy Kidney Tip:
This soft, fluffy rice dish, perfumed with lemongrass, can be eaten as a main course or topped with curry.

Spaghetti and Herb Pesto

- 1 cup fresh basil
- 1/2 cup fresh parsley
- 1/2 cup fresh cilantro
- 1/2 cup fresh mint
- 3 cloves garlic
- 1/4 cup extra-virgin olive oil
- 1 tbsp. balsamic vinegar

- 1 lb. spaghetti cooked according to package directions

Directions

Prep Time: 10 min. | Cook Time: - | Servings: 8

1. Pulse all ingredients (but the spaghetti) in a food processor until smooth.
2. Serve pesto over cooked spaghetti.

Nutrition Facts
(per serving)

Calories: 77.7
Protein: 5.0g
Sodium: 3.1mg
Phosphorus: 1.5mg
Potassium: 59.3mg

Happy Kidney Tip:
I love the smell of whirling herbs when I make this pesto. Add more garlic or a Thai chili if you like a stronger taste.

Tuna Pasta Salad

- 8 oz. cooked rotini pasta
- 3 diced radishes
- 1/4 cup chopped, peeled jicama
- 1/4 cup diced water chestnuts
- 1 can white tuna fish
- 1 tbsp. chopped fresh chives
- 1 tbsp. fresh lemon thyme

Dressing:

- 2 tbsp. lemon juice
- 1 1/2 tsp. dijon mustard
- 1 tsp. canola oil
- 1/8 tsp. minced garlic
- 1/8 tsp. black pepper

Directions

Prep Time: 15 min. | Cook Time: - | Servings: 4

1. Drain tuna.
2. In large bowl, mix all the dressing ingredients together with a wire whisk.
3. To the dressing, add the rest of the ingredients.
4. Combine well and refrigerate for 1 hour.
5. Serve chilled.

Nutrition Facts
(per serving)

Calories: 177
Protein: 9.0g
Sodium: 157.5mg
Phosphorus: 100.0mg
Potassium: 189.0mg

Happy Kidney Tip:
Tuna, remarkably, has the lowest cholesterol content of the fishes. This crunchy salad is tasty and high in Omega 3's.

Red Pepper Sauce Spaghetti

- 1 lb. cooked spaghetti
- 1 chopped red pepper (deseeded)
- 4 red peppers
- 1 large peeled onion, quartered
- 6 cloves peeled garlic
- 1 cup water
- 1 eggplant, cubed
- 2 cubed zucchini
- 2 tsp. sugar
- 1 tbsp. dry oregano
- 1/2 cup chopped fresh basil
- pepper to taste

Directions

Prep Time: 20 min. | Cook Time: 1 1/2 hrs. | Servings: 6

1. Place 4 red peppers on aluminum foil and broil in oven until blistered.
2. Place peppers in plastic bag to sweat them, then remove skins.
3. In a stockpot add all ingredients, (except spaghetti) cover and simmer for 1 ½ hours.
4. With an immersion blender puree the ingredients in the pot.
5. Serve over cooked spaghetti.

Nutrition Facts
(per serving)

Calories: 160.2
Protein: 5.9g
Sodium: 2.5mg
Phosphorus: 7.0mg
Potassium: 158.9mg

Happy Kidney Tip:
This is a super healthy, low-potassium sauce for spaghetti or any pasta. A great alternative to tomatoes and is dazzling with the addition of summer vegetables.

Roasted Onion Garlic Pizza

- 1 pkg. dry yeast
- 2 tbsp. sugar
- 2 tbsp. canola oil
- 1/4 cup tepid water
- 1 1/2 cups rice milk (warm)
- 4 cups all purpose flour

Topping:

- 2 tbsp. minced garlic
- 3 red onions sliced thin
- 2 tsp. dried thyme
- 2 tsp. oregano
- 1 cup mozzarella cheese shredded

- 1 cup cooked chicken shredded
- 1 green pepper sliced thin

Directions

Prep Time: 15 min. | Cook Time: 15 min. | Servings: 4

1. Pre-heat oven to 350°.
2. In a bowl add yeast and water and let stand 5 minutes.
3. Add to yeast, rice milk, oil, sugar and flour to form dough.
4. Knead the dough for 10 minutes.
5. Spray oil into a bowl, add dough and spray the top of the dough.
6. Cover the dough with plastic wrap and let rise for about 30 minutes.
7. Punch dough down and remove from bowl and cut into 4 pieces.
8. Roll out each piece into shape of pizza and put on sprayed pizza sheet.
9. Spread the garlic on the pizza rounds.
10. Next add the spices, onions, pepper, chicken and cheese.
11. Bake in oven for 15 minutes or until dough is browned on bottom.

Nutrition Facts
(per serving)

Calories: 216.7
Protein: 10.3g
Sodium: 89.7mg
Phosphorus: 7.6mg
Potassium: 90.7mg

Happy Kidney Tip:
Don't forget to bring these leftover slices to lunch. Pizza is oh-so-yummy!

Lighter Eggplant Parmesan

- 1 large eggplant
- 1 tbsp. olive oil
- 12 oz. dry-curd cottage cheese
- 1/2 cup parmesan cheese
- 1/4 cup freshly chopped parsley
- 1/4 cup egg product from carton
- 1 cup mozzarella shredded

- 3 cups red pepper sauce (pg. 47)

Directions

Prep Time: 15 min. | Cook Time: 1 1/2 hrs. | Servings: 8

1. Pre-heat oven to 400°.
2. Slice eggplant into 1 inch slices.
3. Put slices on lined cookie sheet and brush both sides with oil.
4. Bake for 30 minutes turning eggplant half-way through and remove from oven.
5. Mix cottage cheese, egg, parsley, and parmesan in a medium bowl.
6. Add a little sauce in the bottom of a 9x12 baking dish and cover the sauce with a layer of roasted eggplant.
7. Top with 1/3 of the cheese mixture, then some mozzarella, then some sauce.
8. Add another layer of eggplant and repeat the steps above until all ingredients are used.
9. Cover with foil and bake for 30 minutes.
10. Remove foil and bake 10 minutes more.
11. Remove from oven and let sit for 10 minutes before cutting.

Nutrition Facts
(per serving)

Calories: 121
Protein: 11.4g
Sodium: 145.5mg
Phosphorus: 3.9mg
Potassium: 34.3mg

Happy Kidney Tip:
This version of eggplant parmesan is healthy, low-fat and kidney friendly. Watch your portions to limit your cheese intake.

Easy Salmon Cakes

- 1 1/2 cups cooked salmon flaked with a fork
- 2 tsp. old bay seasoning
- 1/3 cup egg substitute
- 2 tbsp. mayonnaise
- 3/4 cup panko bread crumbs
- 1 small green pepper finely chopped
- 2 tbsp. chopped fresh chives
- 1 tsp. lemon juice
- canola oil for frying

Directions

Prep Time: 20 min. | Cook Time: 20 min. | Servings: 6

1. Combine all ingredients in a large bowl.
2. Form mixture into 6-8 small patties.
3. On a heated, oiled griddle place patties on medium heat.
4. Cook patties 3 minutes on one side, flip and cook for an additional 3 minutes or until golden brown on both sides.
5. Serve with a squeeze of lemon and tartar sauce.

Nutrition Facts
(per serving)

Calories: 104.2
Protein: 9.9g
Sodium: 86.8mg
Phosphorus: 11.5mg
Potassium: 147.2mg

Happy Kidney Tip:
A light and refreshing meal that can be prepared quickly.

Chicken and Grape Salad

- 1 diced apple
- 1 lb. rotelle pasta cooked (according to package directions)
- 1/2 cup seedless grapes
- 1 cup sliced cooked chicken

Dressing:
- 1/2 cup mayonnaise
- 2 tbsp. sriracha hot sauce
- 1/4 cup light sour cream

Directions
Prep Time: 20 min. | Cook Time: - | Servings: 6

1. Combine dressing ingredients in large bowl and mix well.
2. Add cooked pasta and mix well.
3. Add grapes and apples and mix well.
4. Transfer to serving plates and top with sliced chicken.

Nutrition Facts
(per serving)
Calories: 290.7
Protein: 8.3g
Sodium: 112.3mg
Phosphorus: 7.1mg
Potassium: 91.8mg

Happy Kidney Tip: Fruit and chicken in a salad is luscious…. however, this dressing is so easy to make and really delivers an extra punch.

Fresh Berry Salad

- 3 tbsp. balsamic vinegar

- 2 tbsp. honey

- dash of ground cardamom

- ground pepper

- 1 lb. hulled and quartered strawberries

- 1 pint blueberries

- 1 sprig mint leaves roughly torn

Directions

Prep Time: 15 min. | Cook Time: - | Servings: 4

1. Whisk together in a large bowl the vinegar, honey, pepper, and cardamom.
2. Tumble in the berries and mint leaves.
3. Serve chilled.

Nutrition Facts
(per serving)

Calories: 142.4
Protein: 1.0g
Sodium: 51.5mg
Phosphorus: 3.7mg
Potassium: 394.0mg

Happy Kidney Tip:
Blueberries are good to eat if suffering from a UTI (urinary tract infection). They help restrict the growth of bacteria in the urinary system.

Crispy Baked Asparagus Fries

- 1 lb. asparagus trimmed

- 1/2 cup white flour

- 2 beaten eggs

- 3/4 cup panko breadcrumbs

- 1/4 cup parmesan cheese

- 1/2 tsp. pepper

Directions

Prep Time: 15 min. | Cook Time: 10 min. | Servings: 3

1. Pre-heat oven to 400°F.
2. Dredge the asparagus in the flour.
3. Dip the pieces in beaten egg.
4. Dip in panko mixed with pepper and parmesan cheese.
5. Place on a wire rack placed on cookie sheet and bake for 10 minutes or until golden brown.

Nutrition Facts
(per serving)

Calories: 208.3
Protein: 11.8g
Sodium: 89.7mg
Phosphorus: 18.9mg
Potassium: 556.7mg

Happy Kidney Tip:
This recipe is great because asparagus already is shaped like French fries so lends perfectly to faux French fries.

Szechuan Eggplant

- 2 eggplants
- 3 dried red chilis
- 3 tbsp. olive oil
- 4 minced garlic cloves
- 1/2 inch piece of ginger finely chopped
- 4 scallions sliced crosswise
- 1 tbsp. rice wine

- 1 tsp. sugar
- 1/4 tsp. ground szechuan peppercorns
- 1 tbsp. rice vinegar
- 1 tsp. sesame oil

Directions
Prep Time: 20 min. | Cook Time: 15 min. | Servings: 4

1. Cut eggplants into strips 3 inches long by 1 ½ inches wide.
2. Soak chilis in warm water for 15 minutes.
3. Drain chilis, deseed and cut into slices.
4. Add oil to a wok or skillet and fry eggplant on medium heat for 5 minutes turning when each side is browned.
5. Add garlic, ginger and scallions and cook for 2 minutes.
6. Add rest of ingredients and cook for 2 minutes.
7. Serve hot with a dash of sesame oil for garnish.

Nutrition Facts
(per serving)

Calories: 143.3
Protein: 0.9g
Sodium: 49.5mg
Phosphorus: 2.0mg
Potassium: 154.9mg

Happy Kidney Tip:
This spicy dish is low in potassium and is a great kickstarter for a slow day.

Sauted Veggies and Noodles

- 1 tbsp. olive oil

- 1/4 cup diced red onion

- 3 minced garlic cloves

- 1 cup fresh green beans julienned

- 1 cup carrots julienned with a mandolin

- 2 cups cooked spaghetti

- pinch of saffron

Directions

Prep Time: 15 min. | Cook Time: 5 min. | Servings: 4

1. In a hot, oiled skillet cook onions and garlic for 2 minutes.
2. Add saffron.
3. Add the vegetables, stir to mix, and cook for 2-3 minutes.
4. Add noodles and pepper and toss to combine all ingredients.

Nutrition Facts
(per serving)

Calories: 171.9
Protein: 5.0g
Sodium: 18.0mg
Phosphorus: 4.7mg
Potassium: 186.3mg

Happy Kidney Tip:
This recipe is fun to make using a mandolin with a julienne blade. You can also cut the veggies with a sharp knife. When the dish is done, the veggies are tender crisp like al dente pasta.

Pistou Beef Soup

- 2 small leeks, washed
- 1 small onion peeled
- 2 stalks celery
- 1 medium zucchini
- 1 cup green beans
- 2 carrots, peeled
- 3 tbsp. canola oil
- 1/4 cup water
- 2 quarts beef stock
- 6 roasted red pepper slices
- 4 garlic cloves, peeled
- 1 bunch basil leaves, washed
- 1 bunch parsley, washed
- 1 tsp. ground pepper
- dash hot sauce
- 3 tbsp. olive oil

Directions

Prep Time: 15 min. | Cook Time: 40 min. | Servings: 6

1. Cut the leeks, onion, celery, zucchini, green beans, and carrots into ¼ inch diced cubes.
2. In a large stockpot, combine canola oil and water.
3. On medium heat, cook the veggies, covered, until the water evaporates.
4. To make the pistou, pulse the peppers, basil, parsley, and garlic in a food processor.
5. Drizzle in 3 tbsp. olive oil and pulse til pureed.
6. When veggies are soft in stockpot, add beef stock and simmer for 30 minutes.
7. Add dash or two of hot sauce.
8. Serve soup hot with tablespoon of pistou on top.

Nutrition Facts
(per serving)

Calories: 76.9
Protein: 2.4g
Sodium: 290.6mg
Phosphorus: 4.4mg
Potassium: 334.7mg

Happy Kidney Tip:
Pistou is a traditional French condiment that adds a burst of flavor and this version is kidney-friendly.

Asian Cucumber Salad

- 2 sliced banana peppers
- 1/2 cup diced radishes
- 4 tsp. red diced onion
- 4 tsp. mirin
- 1 tsp. sesame oil
- 1/2 tsp. fresh ginger minced
- 2 tsp. rice wine vinegar

- 4 cups cucumbers partially peeled cut into thin slices
- 1 green onion sliced thin
- 1 tsp. pepper

Directions

Prep Time: 15 min. | Cook Time: - | Servings: 4

1. In large bowl, toss together peppers, radishes, and red onions.
2. In separate bowl, whisk together Mirin, sesame oil, ginger, vinegar, and pepper.
3. Pour dressing over cucumber medley and refrigerate for 2 hours or overnight.
4. Serve with a sprinkling of green onions.

Nutrition Facts
(per serving)

Calories: 34.0
Protein: 0.9g
Sodium: 50.0mg
Phosphorus: 28.3mg
Potassium: 198.0mg

Happy Kidney Tip: Radishes and their juice can cleanse the kidneys and improve renal function. A quick salad to prepare and more delicious the longer it marinates.

Cajun Stuffed Peppers

- 1 cup chopped roasted red peppers
- 6 fresh bell peppers
- 1/2 lb. ground beef
- 1/2 lb. ground pork
- 1/4 cup hot water
- 1 medium onion chopped
- 3 cups cooked white rice
- 1/2 tsp. black pepper
- 1/2 tsp lemon pepper
- 1 tbsp. dried thyme
- 1 tbsp. minced garlic

Directions

Prep Time: 10 min. | Cook Time: 45 min. | Servings: 6

1. Pre-heat oven to 350°F.
2. Bring a large pot of water to a boil and drop in the bell peppers.
3. Boil the peppers for 5 minutes. Remove and drain.
4. Prepare the peppers by removing the stem and removing the seeds.
5. In a large skillet, cook the ground meat over medium heat until it is browned.
6. Add the hot water, roasted red peppers, onions, garlic, and spices.
7. Cook for 5 minutes.
8. Add rice and stir to combine and cook for 3 minutes. Remove from heat and stuff the bell peppers. Put the stuffed peppers in a baking dish and bake, uncovered, for 30 minutes.
9. Serve with a garnish of roasted red peppers.

Nutrition Facts
(per serving)
Calories: 173.5
Protein: 8.8g
Sodium: 27.7mg
Phosphorus: 8.0mg
Potassium: 166.1mg

Happy Kidney Tip:
One of the doctors I worked with gave me this recipe. I didn't think I liked stuffed peppers, but she changed my mind. These are delish!

Stuffed Zucchini

- 4 large zucchini
- 2 tbsp. canola oil
- 1 diced onion
- 1 red bell pepper diced
- 1 cup shredded carrots
- 1 summer squash diced
- 4 matzo broken into pieces
- 1 tsp. dried oregano
- 2 tsp. minced garlic
- 1 tsp. ground pepper
- 1 lb. ground chicken, cooked

Directions

Prep Time: 20 min. | Cook Time: 45 min. | Servings: 8

1. Pre-heat oven to 350°F.
2. Slice zucchini in half, lengthwise, and scoop out insides leaving ¼ inch zucchini on skins.
3. Reserve the insides.
4. Place zucchini halves skin-side down on baking sheet.
5. In a large skillet over medium heat warm the oil.
6. Add the onion and sauté for 3 minutes.
7. Add the zucchini insides, the rest of the veggies, the matzo and the spices.
8. Sauté for 2 minutes.
9. Add the chicken and mix well.
10. Remove from heat and stuff the zucchini with the mixture.
11. Bake for 30 minutes.

Nutrition Facts
(per serving)

Calories: 157
Protein: 9.5g
Sodium: 49.0mg
Phosphorus: 4.4mg
Potassium: 236.1mg

Happy Kidney Tip:
These boats are appealing, healthy, and mouth-watering.

Appetizers

Shrimp Kababs with Chutney

- 2 tbsp. chili powder
- 2 tbsp. garam masala
- 2 tbsp. canola oil
- lemon juice from 2 lemons
- black pepper
- 1 lb. large shrimp shelled, deveined, and tails left on

- 1 cup fresh cilantro
- 1/2 cup fresh mint leaves
- 4 chopped scallions
- 1 thai chili minced fine
- zest of 1 lime
- 2 tbsp. honey
- 2 tbsp. canola oil

- 6-inch skewers (soaked in cold water)

Directions

Prep Time: 10 min. | Cook Time: 5 min. | Servings: 4

1. Whisk together chili powder, garam masala, oil, lemon juice, and pepper in a medium bowl.
2. Add the shrimp, mix and marinate for 15 minutes.
3. In a food processor, combine cilantro, mint, scallions, chili, honey, oil, and lime zest and process to a smooth paste.
4. Thread 4 shrimp onto a skewer so the shrimp lay flat and sprinkle each skewer of shrimp with pepper.
5. On a large grill pan (or outside grill) cook until golden brown and slightly charred on both sides about 1 ½ minutes per side.
6. Serve shrimp with chutney.

Nutrition Facts
(per serving)

Calories: 181.7
Protein: 30.5g
Sodium: 294.3mg
Phosphorus: 17.1mg
Potassium: 370.0mg

Happy Kidney Tip: These spices used to marinate the shrimp are intoxicating. The chutney complements the shrimp with a cooling effect.

Tropical Chicken Salad

- 1/2 cup diced celery
- 1 1/2 cup shredded cooked chicken
- 1 cup peeled and diced apples
- 1 cup drained unsweetened pineapple chunks
- 1/2 cup seedless grapes
- 1 cup diced pears
- 1/2 tsp. sugar
- 2 tbsp. lemon juice
- 1/2 cup mayonnaise
- dash hot sauce
- 1 tsp. pepper
- paprika for garnish

Directions

Prep Time: 20 min. | Cook Time: - | Servings: 4

1. Mix together sugar, juice, mayo, hot sauce, and pepper.
2. In a large bowl mix together rest of ingredients.
3. Add dressing to fruit and chicken and combine well.
4. Serve on a bed of lettuce and sprinkle with paprika.

Nutrition Facts
(per serving)

Calories: 443.8
Protein: 33.1g
Sodium: 245.5mg
Phosphorus: 30.2mg
Potassium: 563.5mg

Happy Kidney Tip:
The bounties of summer star in this satisfying salad!

Pickled Red Onions

- 2 red onions thinly sliced
- 1 cup cider vinegar
- 1/2 cup sugar

Directions

Prep Time: 10 min. | Cook Time: 5 min. | Servings: 6

1. Blanch the onions in a small pan of boiling water for 1 minute and drain in a colander.
2. Return them to a pan and add vinegar and enough cold water to barely cover the onions.
3. Bring to a boil and then simmer the onions for 1 minute.
4. Remove from heat and transfer the brine and onions to a glass jar and chill.
5. The onions will crisp as they cool.

Happy Kidney Tip: These onions are great on burgers and sandwiches and will keep for weeks in the refrigerator.

Zucchini Pancakes

- 4-5 medium zucchini
- 4 eggs
- 2 cloves garlic minced
- 3/4 cup all purpose flour
- 2 tbsp. chopped onion
- pinch red pepper flakes
- 1 tsp. black pepper
- 2 tbsp canola oil

Directions

Prep Time: 15 min. | Cook Time: 20 min. | Servings: 6

1. Coarsely grate zucchini onto kitchen towel.
2. Roll up zucchini in towel and squeeze out excess water.
3. Set aside zucchini to dry further.
4. In a large bowl beat eggs, garlic, onions, and spices.
5. Add flour and mix until moistened.
6. Add zucchini and combine well.
7. Spoon one heaping tablespoon of batter onto a hot greased griddle and spread to a 3" circle.
8. Repeat for each pancake and cook over medium heat 3 minutes on each side.
9. Pancakes should be a golden brown.

Nutrition Facts
(per serving)

Calories: 132.6
Protein: 6.3g
Sodium: 50.0mg
Phosphorus: 11.0mg
Potassium: 231.9mg

Happy Kidney Tip: The glistening surface of these culinary marvels are delightful to look at and delicious to eat. These pancakes freeze well and can be reheated in a hot oven til crispy!

Strawberry Applsauce

- 2 apples cored and cut into chunky pieces

- 1 cup fresh or frozen strawberries

- 2 cups water

- 1 tbsp. lemon juice

- 1 tsp. honey

- 1 tsp cinnamon

Directions

Prep Time: 10 min. | Cook Time: 30 min. | Servings: 16

1. Put all the ingredients into a large saucepan.
2. Bring to a boil over medium heat.
3. Lower the heat and simmer for about 30 minutes.
4. Remove from heat and cool for 10 minutes.
5. Puree in blender...if thick add a little more water.

Nutrition Facts
(per serving)

Calories: 73.3
Protein: 0.4g
Sodium: 7.0mg
Phosphorus: 0.4mg
Potassium: 170.5mg

Happy Kidney Tip:
Try this luscious sauce with our herb crusted pork tenderloin (pg. 111).

Zesty Deviled Eggs

- 4 ten- minute hard-boiled eggs

- 1 tbsp. chopped celery

- 1/2 tsp. dry mustard

- 1/2 tsp. vinegar

- 1 tbsp. mayonnaise

- 1 tbsp. finely chopped onion

- paprika for garnish

Directions

Prep Time: 15 min. | Cook Time: - | Servings: 4

1. Cut eggs in half lengthwise.
2. Remove yolks and place in a bowl.
3. Place remaining ingredients in bowl with yolks and mash with a fork.
4. Refill eggs and sprinkle with paprika

Nutrition Facts
(per serving)

Calories: 124
Protein: 6.2g
Sodium: 97.6mg
Phosphorus: 0.4mg
Potassium: 50.5mg

Happy Kidney Tip: These are easy to eat zesty appetizers. Don't cook the eggs too long or a ring of green around the yolks will surprise you when you cut them open.

Shrimp Spring Rolls

- 1 ounce rice vermicelli noodles
- 1 tsp. fresh ginger finely chopped
- 2 green onions finely chopped
- 2 carrots grated
- 1/2 cup cabbage grated
- 1 tbsp. chopped mint leaves
- 1 tbsp. chives

- 24 cooked med-sized shrimp (cut in half lengthwise)
- 24 spring roll wrappers

Dipping Sauce:
- 1/4 cup sugar
- 1/4 cup rice vinegar
- 2 fresh red chilis

Directions

Prep Time: 30 min. | Cook Time: - | Servings: 24

1. In a small saucepan, boil the sugar and vinegar with 2 tbsp. water.
2. Stir in the chilis and set aside.
3. Soak the noodles according to package directions and rinse well.
4. Cut noodles in short lengths with scissors.
5. In large bowl, combine ginger, green onions, carrots, cabbage, mint, and chives.
6. Place a moistened spring roll wrapper on a work surface.
7. Place a spoonful of filling in middle and top with 2 shrimp.
8. Fold in each side of the wrapper, and then roll up tightly. Brush the end of wrapper with a dab of water and seal.
9. Repeat until all filling is used.
10. Serve with chili dipping sauce.

Nutrition Facts
(per serving)
Calories: 103.9
Protein: 1.4g
Sodium: 574.0mg
Phosphorus: 0.9mg
Potassium: 22.2mg

Happy Kidney Tip: These dainty spring rolls make perfect party finger food.

Cranberry Ginger Chutney

- 1 cup red onion, diced
- 1 tsp. canola oil
- 1 tbsp. grated fresh ginger
- 1 cup apple with skin finely chopped
- 1 tsp. pepper
- 2 cups cranberries
- 2 tbsp. apple cider vinegar
- 2 tbsp. raspberry jam
- lime zest

Directions

Prep Time: 10 min. | Cook Time: 45 min. | Servings: 8

1. In a large skillet, cook red onions in oil over medium heat until soft or about 8 minutes.
2. Add the rest of the ingredients and cook for another 5 minutes.
3. Reduce heat to a simmer and cook for 15 minutes or until sauce thickens.
4. Remove from heat and place in a serving bowl and top with zest.

Nutrition Facts
(per serving)

Calories: 44
Protein: 0.4g
Sodium: 3.4mg
Phosphorus: 10.7mg
Potassium: 73.6mg

Happy Kidney Tip: This compote is pleasing to look at and the ginger adds a nice punch!

- 1 cup blackberries

- 2 sprigs mint leaves

- 1 cup seedless red grapes

- 2 cups cubed watermelon

- 1 tbsp. honey

- 1 tbsp. lime juice

Directions

Prep Time: 10 min. | Cook Time: - | Servings: 6

1. Combine all ingredients in a large bowl.
2. Place in freezer just until fruit is somewhat frozen.
3. Serve in cups for a crunchy surprise.

Nutrition Facts
(per serving)

Calories: 50.3
Protein: 0.6g
Sodium: 1.3mg
Phosphorus: 1.3mg
Potassium: 134.0mg

Happy Kidney Tip:
This appetizer is a great time saver as it can be made the night before and served to an admiring audience.

Garlicky Nettle Pesto

- 1/2 lb. nettles
- 5 garlic cloves peeled
- 1/2 cup unsalted pumpkin seeds
- ground pepper
- 1 tbsp. lemon juice
- 1 1/4 cups extra-virgin olive oil
- 2 tbsp. parmesan cheese

Directions

Prep Time: 15 min. | Cook Time: - | Servings: 8

1. In a large pot of boiling water add the nettles directly from the bag and cook for 2 minutes.
2. Drain in a colander.
3. Place nettles on a dishtowel and wring out as much water as possible.
4. In a food processor whirl the garlic, seeds, and pepper.
5. Add the nettles and lemon juice and whirl another 2 minutes.
6. With the machine running, add the oil.
7. Add the cheese last and pulse briefly.

Nutrition Facts
(per serving)

Calories: 55
Protein: 2.6g
Sodium: 36.0mg
Phosphorus: 0.0mg
Potassium: 0.0mg

Happy Kidney Tip:
This vibrant green pesto is very healthy and is so low in phosphorous and potassium. This is delightful served on cucumber rounds! Nettles are diuretics in that they flush out the kidneys.

Crunchy Potato Croquettes

- 4 medium "leached" potato cooked and peeled

- 1 tbsp. butter

- 1 tbsp. rice milk

- 1 tsp. pepper

- 1 beaten egg

- 1 cup white bread crumbs

- 2 tbsp. canola oil

Directions

Prep Time: 15 min. | Cook Time: 20 min. | Servings: 4

1. Mash potatoes with milk, butter and pepper.
2. Form cooled potatoes into balls with your hands.
3. Dip balls in beaten egg.
4. Next, roll balls in bread crumbs.
5. Then place balls in hot oiled skillet and fry until golden brown.

Nutrition Facts
(per serving)

Calories: 322.1
Protein: 7.5g
Sodium: 399.7mg
Phosphorus: 13.5mg
Potassium: 233.5mg

Happy Kidney Tip:
These scrumptious, crispy balls are heavenly dipped in our red-pepper sauce!

Vegetarian Summer Rolls

- 1 ounce rice vermicelli noodles
- 2 zucchinis shredded
- 2 carrots shredded
- 2 shallots finely chopped
- 2 small cucumbers peeled and diced
- 1/3 cup fresh basil chopped
- ½ cup fresh cilantro chopped

- 24 spring roll wrappers

Dipping Sauce:

- 1/4 cup sugar
- 1/4 cup rice vinegar
- 2 fresh red chilis

Directions

Prep Time: 30 min. | Cook Time: - | Servings: 24

1. Place sugar, vinegar and 2 tbsp. water in saucepan and boil gently.
2. Remove from heat, add chilis and set aside.
3. In large bowl combine all rest of ingredients (except wrappers).
4. Place a moistened wrapper on a work surface.
5. Put spoonful of filling in center and fold to encase bringing corner to corner.
6. Fold in sides and roll up tightly. Brush end with water to seal.
7. Repeat until all filling is used.
8. Serve with dipping sauce.

Nutrition Facts
(per serving)
Calories: 94.5
Protein: 0.2g
Sodium: 562.6mg
Phosphorus: 0.5mg
Potassium: 34.0mg

Happy Kidney Tip:
A great vegetarian hand roll kicked up in flavor with an appealing sauce!

Entrees

Hot and Sour Noodles

- 2 tbsp. canola oil
- 4 cloves garlic, finely chopped
- 2 inch piece of ginger, peeled and grated
- 1 medium green chili, seeded and finely chopped
- 1 medium red chili, seeded and finely chopped
- 1/4 cup rice vinegar
- 1/8 cup chili oil

- 1 cup asparagus
- 3 zucchini, sliced into thin strips
- 1 lb. fresh noodles, cooked
- 1 bunch chopped fresh cilantro
- toasted sesame oil

Directions

Prep Time: 20 min. | Cook Time: 10 min. | Servings: 4

1. Heat a skillet or wok over med-high heat and add the oil.
2. Stir-fry the garlic, ginger, and chilis for 1 minute.
3. Add the vinegar and chili oil and reduce to a simmer.
4. In a large pot of boiling water, add the asparagus and zucchini.
5. Cook for 2 minutes and drain.
6. Add veggies and noodles to wok and cook for 1 minute so all is dressed with the fragrant oil.
7. Transfer to a serving platter and garnish with cilantro and sesame oil.

Nutrition Facts
(per serving)
Calories: 415.2
Protein: 7.6g
Sodium: 362.4mg
Phosphorus: 4.0mg
Potassium: 200.7mg

Happy Kidney Tip:
Asparagus improves urine flow and cleanses the kidneys and bladder. This is a spicy dish and loaded with flavor.

Pork and Plum Tenderloin

- 12 oz. pork tenderloin
- 2 tsp. olive oil
- 1 cup grapes
- 2 garlic cloves, minced
- 3 fresh plums, pitted and chopped
- 3 tbsp. lemon juice
- 2 tbsp. sugar
- 1 seeded jalapeno pepper
- 1 tsp. grated fresh ginger
- 1/2 cup blueberries

Directions

Prep Time: 20 min. | Cook Time: 40 min. | Servings: 4

1. Pre-heat oven to 400 degrees F.
2. Brush tenderloin with oil.
3. Rub garlic into meat and place meat on rack in a shallow roasting pan.
4. Roast for 30 minutes or until internal temperature is 160 degrees.
5. For salsa, pulse plums, grapes, sugar, jalapeno, lemon juice, and ginger in a food processor.
6. Process til roughly chopped.
7. Transfer to a small saucepan and cook over medium heat for 2 minutes.
8. To serve, slice meat and serve with warm salsa.

Nutrition Facts
(per serving)
Calories: 242.8
Protein: 26.6g
Sodium: 57.5mg
Phosphorus: 26.9mg
Potassium: 536.7mg

Happy Kidney Tip: This sweet and colorful salsa is served over low-calorie pork tenderloin. Yum!

Rosemary Chicken and Noodles

- 16 oz. cooked egg noodles
- 1/2 cup sliced scallions
- 1/2 cup frozen petite green peas
- 3 tbsp. sesame oil
- 2 tbsp. canola oil
- 2 tbsp. finely chopped fresh rosemary
- 1 tsp. minced garlic
- 1/2 cup diced onion
- 2 tbsp. lemon juice
- 2 tbsp. honey
- 2 cups cooked shredded chicken

Directions

Prep Time: 20 min. | Cook Time: - | Servings: 6

1. Mix together sesame oil, lemon juice, and honey and set aside.
2. In skillet, sauté onions and garlic in oil until carmelized.
3. In large bowl mix together noodles, peas, and scallions.
4. Add onions, sesame oil mixture, and chicken to the noodle mixture.
5. Toss well and serve.

Nutrition Facts
(per serving)
Calories: 172.9
Protein: 12.3g
Sodium: 35.4mg
Phosphorus: 12.0mg
Potassium: 134.8mg

Happy Kidney Tip: Rosemary is an herb that supports brain health and memory. This tasty dish can be enjoyed by all.

Grilled Shrimp Over Rice

- 1 lb. fresh shrimp shelled and deveined
- 3 cups cooked white rice

Marinade:

- 2 tbsp. olive oil
- 1 tsp. grated lime peel
- 2 tbsp. lime juice
- 1/2 cup pineapple juice

- 1/4 tsp. red pepper flakes
- 2 minced garlic cloves

Directions

Prep Time: 10 min. | Cook Time: 15 min. | Servings: 4

1. Put all marinade ingredients in a resealable plastic bag.
2. Add shrimp and shake to coat all the shrimp.
3. Seal bag and refrigerate for 30 minutes.
4. Remove from refrigerator and place shrimp on hot griddle.
5. Cook shrimp 3 minutes on each side, or until shrimp are no longer pink.
6. Serve over hot rice.

Nutrition Facts
(per serving)
Calories: 368.8
Protein: 27.2g
Sodium: 254.5mg
Phosphorus: 21.2mg
Potassium: 284.8mg

Happy Kidney Tip:
A squeeze of lemon over the shrimp finishes off this scrumptious dish.

Fancy Rigatoni

- 3 cups cooked rigatoni pasta (or any shape)
- 8 oz. chicken breast
- 2 cloves garlic chopped
- 2 tbsp. canola oil
- 1/2 cup chopped green onions
- 1/2 cup chopped red pepper
- 1/4 tsp. cayenne pepper
- 1/2 cup white wine
- 1 cup salt-free chicken broth
- bunch fresh basil torn into pieces
- bunch fresh parsley chopped fine
- paprika

Directions
Prep Time: 10 min. | Cook Time: 20 min. | Servings: 4

1. Sauté garlic in oil in large skillet.
2. Cut chicken into strips.
3. Brown with garlic for 5 minutes.
4. Add remaining ingredients and simmer for 20 minutes covered.
5. Remove from heat and toss in cooked pasta, and herbs.
6. Serve with paprika sprinkled on top.

Nutrition Facts
(per serving)
Calories: 335.0
Protein: 19.0g
Sodium: 164.0mg
Phosphorus: 196.0mg
Potassium: 122.0mg

Happy Kidney Tip:
This is a comforting casserole with easily digested ingredients.

Herb Crusted Pork Tenderloin

- 4 lb. boneless pork loin untrimmed

- 2 tbsp. olive oil

- 4 cloves garlic, minced

- 1 tsp. dried thyme

- 1 tsp. dried basil

- 1 tsp. dried rosemary

Directions

Prep Time: 10 min. | Cook Time: 1 hr. 45 min. | Servings: 6

1. Pre-heat oven to 450°F.
2. Place the pork loin on a rack in a roasting pan.
3. Combine the remaining ingredients in a small bowl.
4. Rub the pork loin with the paste.
5. Roast the pork for 30 minutes.
6. Reduce heat to 375°F and roast for an additional hour or until internal temperature reaches 160°F.
7. Allow to sit for 20 minutes before carving.

Nutrition Facts
(per serving)

Calories: 219.4
Protein: 28.9g
Sodium: 61.7mg
Phosphorus: 28.2mg
Potassium: 434.0mg

Happy Kidney Tip: Impress friends and family with this spectacular roast especially when covered with our cranberry ginger chutney.

Sweet and Sour Pork

- 2 cups pork cooked and cubed
- 2 tbsp. canola oil
- 3 cups cooked white rice
- 2 carrots sliced thin lengthwise
- 1 red bell pepper sliced thin
- 1 yellow bell pepper sliced thin
- 1 cup pineapple in chunks
- 2 spring onions finely sliced

Sweet and Sour Sauce:

- 4 oz. pineapple juice
- 4 oz. pineapple
- 3 tbsp. fresh lime juice

Directions

Prep Time: 15 min. | Cook Time: 15 min. | Servings: 4

1. To make the sauce, blend together pineapple juice, lime juice, and pineapples in a blender.
2. Whiz to a paste.
3. Heat a wok or pan over high heat and add the oil and pork.
4. Lightly brown on all sides and remove pork from wok.
5. Add veggies (except spring onions) to wok and lightly brown on all sides.
6. Pour in sauce in blender and cover pan.
7. Cook for 3 minutes and uncover.
8. Add pork and simmer 3 more minutes.
9. Serve over hot rice.
10. Garnish with spring onions.

Nutrition Facts
(per serving)

Calories: 388.3
Protein: 17.9g
Sodium: 47.2mg
Phosphorus: 20.1mg
Potassium: 454.2mg

Happy Kidney Tip:
Pineapples have bromelain which is an enzyme that helps fight infections and has anti-inflammatory properties. They also have a diuretic nature in helping the kidneys function.

Chicken with Cauliflower Mash

- 1 tbsp. fresh rosemary
- 1 tbsp. fresh thyme
- 1 tbsp. softened butter
- 6 minced garlic cloves
- 2 large skinless, boneless, chicken breasts
- 6 cups cauliflower florets
- 3 oz. reduced fat cream cheese
- 1 tbsp. olive oil
- 1 tbsp. parmesan cheese grated
- 1/4 cup water
- paprika

Directions

Prep Time: 10 min. | Cook Time: 30 min. | Servings: 4

1. In a small bowl, combine herbs, butter and garlic.
2. Place each chicken breast between 2 pieces of plastic wrap and pound chicken lightly to ½ inch thick with a meat mallet.
3. Cut each chicken piece in half crosswise.
4. Place cauliflower in steamer basket and over boiling water, steam cauliflower for 10 minutes.
5. In a food processor, combine cauliflower and cream cheese. Pulse til smooth.
7. In a large griddle, heat oil over medium heat.
8. Add chicken and cook for 3 minutes.
9. Turn chicken and top with herb mixture and parmesan cheese.
10. Add water to griddle, cover, and simmer for 10 minutes or until chicken is no longer pink in middle. (170 degrees F.)
11. To serve, spoon cauliflower mash onto plate and top with chicken.
12. Sprinkle with paprika.

Nutrition Facts
(per serving)
Calories: 154.4
Protein: 14.0g
Sodium: 63.4mg
Phosphorus: 16.2mg
Potassium: 414.1mg

Happy Kidney Tip: Rich, creamy, and satisfying....this is especially delicious on a cold day!

Spicey Pineapple Chicken

- 4-5 oz. boneless, skinless, chicken breasts
- 20 oz. can pineapple chunks
- 2 tsp. chopped garlic
- 1 tsp. dijon mustard
- 1 tsp. wasabi paste
- 1/2 cup chopped cilantro
- 1/4 cup chopped red onion

Directions

Prep Time: 10 min. | Cook Time: 15 min. | Servings: 4

1. Mix pineapple juice from can with garlic, mustard and wasabi in large bowl.
2. Add chicken pieces.
3. Cover and marinate in refrigerator overnight.
4. Place chicken in skillet and cover.
5. Cook on medium heat for 15 minutes or until chicken is no longer pink inside.
6. Add onion, pineapple and cilantro and mix well.
7. Garnish with cilantro.

Nutrition Facts
(per serving)

Calories: 123.7
Protein: 8.6g
Sodium: 74.1mg
Phosphorus: 7.8mg
Potassium: 225.0mg

Happy Kidney Tip:
Colorful and spicy...
I love this dish.

Cranberry Meatloaf

- 2 lb. lean ground beef
- 1 cup white breadcrumbs
- 1/4 cup egg substitute
- 2 tsp. dry mustard
- 1 tsp. dried sage
- 1/2 tsp. dried rosemary
- 1 tsp. thyme

- 1/3 cup jellied cranberry sauce

Directions

Prep Time: 10 min. | Cook Time: 1 hr. | Servings: 8

1. Pre-heat oven to 350°F.
2. In large bowl, mix together all ingredients.
3. Place mix into 2 greased loaf pans or 1 large loaf pan.
4. Bake 1 hour and remove from oven.
5. Cool before slicing.

Nutrition Facts
(per serving)
Calories: 283.5
Protein: 23.1g
Sodium: 193.9mg
Phosphorus: 17.8mg
Potassium: 292.4mg

Happy Kidney Tip:
Serve this delicious meatloaf over potato cauliflower mash...recipe follows.

Cauliflower Mash

- 2 cups "leached" potatoes
- 2 cups cauliflower florets
- 2 tbsp. softened butter
- 3/4 cup tepid milk
- 1 tsp. ground black pepper

Directions

Prep Time: 5 min. | Cook Time: 10 min. | Servings: 4

1. Cut potatoes into quarters.
2. Break apart cauliflower.
3. Add veggies to a large pot of boiling water.
4. Cook til veggies are tender, about 10 minutes.
5. Remove from heat, and drain.
6. Add milk, butter and pepper.
7. With an immersion blender, cream veggies.
8. Serve hot.

Nutrition Facts
(per serving)

Calories: 158.4
Protein: 5.2g
Sodium: 384.7mg
Phosphorus: 13.7mg
Potassium: 414.2mg

Happy Kidney Tip:
This delicious mash can served as a side or as a meal! So good!

Desserts

Turnover Delights

- 1 1/4 lbs. tart apples
- 1 cup sliced strawberries
- 3 tbsp. sugar
- 1 tbsp. all purpose flour
- 1/4 tsp. ground cinnamon
- 1/8 tsp. ground nutmeg
- 1 pkg. (2 sheets) frozen puff pastry, defrosted
- egg wash (1 egg beaten with 1 tbsp. water)

Directions

Prep Time: 20 min. | Cook Time: 20 min. | Servings: 8

1. Pre-heat oven to 400°F.
2. Peel and core apples and cut into ¾ inch dice.
3. Add the strawberries, sugar, flour, and spices.
4. Flour a board and lightly roll each sheet of pastry to a 12x12 inch square.
5. Cut each square into 4 smaller squares.
6. Brush the edges of the squares with the egg wash and place tablespoon full of apple filling in center.
7. Fold pastry diagonally over apples and press edges with a fork to seal tightly.
8. Transfer to a lined sheet pan.
9. Brush top with egg wash and sprinkle with sugar. Make 2 small slits on top of each turnover.
10. Bake for 20 minutes til brown and puffed.

Nutrition Facts
(per serving)

Calories: 139.0
Protein: 2.0g
Sodium: 50.2mg
Phosphorus: 2.8mg
Potassium: 178.1mg

Happy Kidney Tip:
Super simple...super delicious!

Peaches and Cream Puffs

- 1/2 cup butter
- 1 cup water
- 1/4 tsp. ground cinnamon
- 1/8 tsp. ground nutmeg
- 1/8 tsp. ground ginger
- 1 cup all purpose flour
- 4 eggs

- 1 container non-dairy whipped cream
- 8 oz. pkg. softened cream cheese
- 2 tbsp. peach preserves
- 1/2 tsp. almond extract
- 2 peaches peeled and chopped

Directions

Prep Time: 30 min. | Cook Time: 45 min. | Servings: 12

1. Pre-heat oven to 400°F.
2. In a medium saucepan, over medium heat, add butter, water, and spices. Bring to a boil.
3. Add flour and stir vigorously.
4. Cook and stir til mixture forms a ball and remove from heat.
5. Cool 10 minutes, and then add eggs, one at a time beating continuously til smooth.
6. Drop batter by heaping spoonfuls onto lined baking sheet, about 3 inches apart.
7. Bake 30 minutes or until golden brown. Cool on a wire rack.
8. In a medium bowl, mix together whipped cream, cream cheese, peach preserves and almond extract.
9. Stir in chopped peaches.
10. To assemble...cut off top one fourth of each puff. Remove soft dough from inside.
12. Fill with peach mixture.
13. Replace tops and sprinkle with powdered sugar if desired.

Nutrition Facts
(per serving)
Calories: 227.1
Protein: 4.8g
Sodium: 82.1mg
Phosphorus: 6.9mg
Potassium: 95.7mg

Happy Kidney Tip: These delights can be stored in refrigerator 1 hour before serving.

Scrumptious Sugar Cookies

- 2 3/4 cup flour

- 2 tsp. cream of tartar

- 1 tsp. baking soda

- 1 1/2 cups sugar

- 1 cup softened butter

- 2 large eggs

- 2 tsp. vanilla extract

Directions

Prep Time: 20 min. | Cook Time: 10 min. | Servings: 24

1. Pre-heat oven to 350°F.
2. Mix together flour, baking soda, cream of tartar in large bowl.
3. In medium bowl, beat together sugar and butter with electric mixer.
4. Gradually add flour mixture to sugar and butter.
5. Put dough in refrigerator for 1 hour.
6. Remove from refrigerator and shape dough into 1-2 inch balls with your hands.
7. Place 2 inches apart on lined baking sheets.
8. Bake 10 minutes or until lightly browned.
9. Cool on wire racks.

Nutrition Facts
(per serving)

Calories: 167.4
Protein: 2.0g
Sodium: 108.8mg
Phosphorus: 2.5mg
Potassium: 62.2mg

Happy Kidney Tip: These are mouth-watering buttery cookies made with no baking powder!

Baked Apple and Pear Slices

- 2 cups peeled sliced pears

- 2 cups peeled, cored, sliced apples

- 3 tbsp. sugar

- 1 tsp. cinnamon

- 1 tbsp. maple syrup

Directions

Prep Time: 10 min. | Cook Time: 5 min. | Servings: 2

1. Put fruit in a glass bowl.
2. Add sugar and cinnamon.
3. Bake in microwave oven for 5 minutes on high heat.
4. Test for doneness with a fork.
5. Remove from microwave and mix in maple syrup.

Nutrition Facts
(per serving)
Calories: 421.8
Protein: 2.0g
Sodium: 4.9mg
Phosphorus: 3.6mg
Potassium: 823.0mg

Happy Kidney Tip:
Try topping this quick dessert with non-dairy whipped cream. Yum!!

Pear Streusel Pie

- 1 frozen dough crust partially thawed
- 6 cups pears peeled, cored, and chopped
- 1 1/2 tbsp. cornstarch
- 1/4 cup packed brown sugar
- 1/4 cup maple syrup
- 1 tbsp. lemon juice
- 1/2 tsp. ground ginger

Topping:
- 1/2 cup flour
- 2/3 cup old-fashioned oats
- 1/2 cup packed brown sugar
- 1/3 cup cold butter cut into ¼ inch pieces

Directions
Prep Time: 20 min. | Cook Time: 1 hr. | Servings: 8

1. Pre-heat oven to 400°F.
2. In a large bowl, toss together pears, cornstarch, sugar, maple syrup and lemon juice.
3. Place this pear mixture into pie shell.
4. Bake for 40 minutes.
5. Remove from oven and reduce temperature to 350 degrees F.
6. In a medium bowl, add topping ingredients and combine well using your hands to form a crumbly texture.
7. Top pie with mixture and return to oven for 15 minutes.
8. Cool for 1 hour.

Nutrition Facts
(per serving)

Calories: 256.2
Protein: 2.3g
Sodium: 23.9mg
Phosphorus: 3.2mg
Potassium: 233.2mg

Happy Kidney Tip:
I love crumb toppings on pies and this is a change using pears, from traditional apple pie.

Blueberry Caramel Sauce

- 1 cup blueberries

- 1 cup sugar

- 1/4 cup water

- 1 tbsp. lemon juice

Directions

Prep Time: 10 min. | Cook Time: 20 min. | Servings: 8

1. Place blueberries in food processor and puree.
2. In a small saucepan, heat sugar and water over medium heat for 2 minutes.
3. Simmer this mixture for 10 minutes, stirring frequently, until a dark amber color has been reached.
4. Remove from heat and mix in blueberry puree.
5. Return to heat and simmer for 3 minutes.
6. Strain the sauce through a sieve to remove any solids.
7. Mix in lemon juice and let cool.

Nutrition Facts
(per serving)

Calories: 106.9
Protein: 0.1g
Sodium: 1.1mg
Phosphorus: 0.2mg
Potassium: 23.4mg

Happy Kidney Tip:
A caramel sauce with an amazing aroma of sweet blueberries... this sauce will thicken as it cools.

Blueberry-Lemon Cheesecake

- 1/2 cup sugar
- 1 1/2 cups flour
- 1/2 tsp. cream of tartar
- 1/8 tsp. baking soda
- 1/2 cup cold butter
- 1 large egg, separated
- 1 large egg, separated

- 1 tbsp. lemon zest
- 2 cups dry-curd cottage cheese
- 1/2 cup sugar
- 3 tbsp. flour
- 2 tsp. vanilla extract
- 2 eggs and 1 egg white
- 4 tbsp. lemon juice

- 1 cup blueberries

Directions
Prep Time: 20 min. | Cook Time: 45 min. | Servings: 12

1. Pre-heat oven to 350°F.
2. In a large mixing bowl, combine sugar, flour, cream of tartar, and baking soda and stir to combine.
3. Add butter and using your hands, mix into crumbly texture.
4. Add egg yolk and combine.
5. Press the crumbly mixture into greased 8x8 baking dish.
6. Bake for 10 minutes and remove from oven.
7. In a food processor, pulse the cottage cheese til smooth.
8. Add eggs, vanilla, lemon juice and zest and pulse until smooth.
9. Add flour and pulse just to combine. Pour mixture into baking dish.
11. Sprinkle blueberries over top.
12. Bake 45 minutes. (filling should be lightly brown and jiggles in center when shaken)
13. Remove and let cool completely and refrigerate overnight.

Nutrition Facts
(per serving)

Calories: 236.8
Protein: 7.9g
Sodium: 75.5mg
Phosphorus: 4.5mg
Potassium: 71.3mg

Happy Kidney Tip:
This is a creamy, satisfying dessert for your sweet-tooth and is elevated to grandeur with our blueberry caramel sauce. (pg. 135)

Vanilla Pudding Sundae

- 1 quart milk
- 2/3 cup sugar
- 1/3 cup cornstarch
- 1 egg
- 3 tbsp. butter
- 2 tsp. vanilla extract
- 4 graham crackers

- 1 cup crushed raspberries
- 1 container non-dairy whipped topping

Directions

Prep Time: 15 min. | Cook Time: 10 min. | Servings: 8

1. In a saucepan, heat milk until bubbles form around edges.
2. In a small bowl, whisk together sugar, cornstarch and egg.
3. Cool milk and whisk in sugar mixture gradually.
4. Continue to cook over med-low heat until pudding coats the back of a spoon
(do not boil).
5. Remove from heat and add vanilla and butter.
6. Stir to combine and cool.
7. Refrigerate overnight.
8. To prepare: layer a glass with crushed graham crackers, followed by pudding,
followed by raspberries, followed by pudding.
9. Top with whipped cream.

Nutrition Facts
(per serving)
Calories: 196.9
Protein: 5.4g
Sodium: 81.8mg
Phosphorus: 13.6mg
Potassium: 204.3mg

Happy Kidney Tip:
This easy-to-prepare dessert is a feast for the eyes and palate!

Made in the USA
Middletown, DE
19 February 2015